Best wishes,
Michael J Cook

Michael James Cook

SELECTED POEMS
TAKE YOUR PICK

MEREO
Cirencester

Mereo Books

1A The Wool Market Dyer Street Cirencester Gloucestershire GL7 2PR
An imprint of Memoirs Publishing www.mereobooks.com

SELECTED POEMS: TAKE YOUR PICK: 978-1-86151-891-0

First published in Great Britain in 2017
by Mereo Books, an imprint of Memoirs Publishing

The address for Memoirs Publishing Group Limited can be found at
www.memoirspublishing.com

The Memoirs Publishing Group Ltd Reg. No. 7834348

The Memoirs Publishing Group supports both The Forest Stewardship Council®
(FSC®) and the PEFC® leading international forest-certification organisations. Our
books carrying both the FSC label and the PEFC® and are printed on FSC®-certified
paper. FSC® is the only forest-certification scheme supported by the leading
environmental organisations including Greenpeace. Our paper procurement policy
can be found at www.memoirspublishing.com/environment

Typeset in 12/18pt Century Schoolbook
by Wiltshire Associates Publisher Services Ltd. Printed and bound in Great Britain
by Printondemand-Worldwide, Peterborough PE2 6XD

Also by Michael James Cook:

NON-FICTION
Have You Ever Thought? (Covenant Pub. Co. Ltd, London, 1961)

POETRY
Stepping Stones (Outposts Publications, 1975)
Reflecting in the Sun (Outposts Publications, 1976)
Of Faith And Fortune (Outposts Publications, 1977)
O Didaskalos (New Millennium, 1997)
Collected Poems 1959–2014 (Troubador Publishing Co. 2015)

To my daughters Sam and Jo, with much love.

ABOUT THE AUTHOR

Michael James Cook was born in North Reddish, Stockport, Cheshire and was educated at Stockport School and the universities of Durham, Bristol and Exeter. A promising career in professional sport was dashed at an early age by a serious knee injury. He was an ordinand of the Church of England and a full-time Youth Leader in Bristol. He was the first full-time Teacher/Youth and Community Leader to be appointed in Cheshire. He also taught Religious and Social Education in secondary modern, comprehensive and grammar schools in Devon, Durham, Essex and Somerset for almost thirty years. When he took early retirement from teaching, he and his wife owned and ran the village shop at Kirkby Mallory in Leicestershire for ten years. He took the F.A. Coaching course when he was a young man and was for many years a part-time soccer scout for a number of Football League clubs; soccer remaining the first love of his life. His many interests, apart from writing poetry, include sport, theology, geology, philately and preserved steam railways. He is a published author, photographer and songwriter.

*"Like a photo without a caption,
a poem will mean different things
to different people; sometimes more,
sometimes less, than the poet intended".*

Michael J. Cook

CONTENTS

INTRODUCTION

This is a collection of best-liked poems of mine selected by others, including family members, friends, acquaintances, teaching colleagues and pupils past and present of Stockport School and Axminster Secondary School, as well as members of the general public. A total of 410 votes were cast to find the top 100 from a list of 240 poems. The working title for the collection was 'Simply The Best' but it was changed to 'Take Your Pick', as it was thought to be more inclusive and less contentious by inviting participation from the reader. One could dispute that the poems chosen were actually my best, so the criteria was changed to what the selectors chose, for whatever reasons, to be their favourite poems. Most have been published previously in magazines, newspapers and anthologies, but there are a few new ones which haven't and a few others which have been revised. I hope the reader really will find that there is something for everyone to enjoy in this collection.

Michael James Cook
Hinckley 2018

FOR YOU MY LOVE

For you my love, words from my pen will flow for ever,
Scribing time-eternal thoughts which may seem clever.
Come to my side and sit with me, fair maiden still.
You are my hope, for helpless is my will.
There is a reason for the twisted tortured way I feel;
I'm just a dreamer, I cannot comprehend what's real.
There is but one journey's end to each upon the earth;
Our bodies are a-dying from the moment of our birth.
So when the testing comes, I'll stay your fears,
Stand firm throughout and shed no mournful tears.
And when the raging storm has passed you by,
If you should turn and chance your eye,
You'll find me standing by your side,
For love-found moments never die.

1971

HAPPY ANNIVERSARY

I could wax lyrical with exaggerated ease
Describing our past five decades shared.
Though my words would surely easily please
They could not justify how much we've cared.

The day we met, which changed our lives for good,
Lives long in the mind where memories hide.
A chance encounter in the twinkling of an eye, we stood
In a garden of Eden, where lovers' paths collide.

Whose was the hand which guided both our steps?
What arrows of desire triggered our transformation?
Mesmerised, we tasted love, its whims and depths.
Virgin kisses sealed our quest for further exploration.

Enforced partings and separations obstructed our way,
Knots of emotion bound us ever closer together.
Love letters writ and posted each passing day,
Containing our hopes and dreams, whatever the weather.

Outside the church, camera flash bulbs shed some light,
All shrouded in mist like the fog on the Tyne,
You posed on that freezing winter's day, turned night,
My Geordie angel so bright and sublime.

We tied the bonds and vowed we'd never fall.
We tried to overcome the wrongs which God forbids.
We toiled to do our best for one and all,
To make the world a better place by what we did.

As years passed by and long days became short,
We entered the Twilight Zone with fading sight.
The sword of Damocles, an ever-present thought;
Uncertainty and dread with sleepless nights.

Tiredness has become our daily cloak and shroud,
While seasons and festivals slowly lose their shine.
Peace is all we seek when others grow too loud.
In truth, our love is stronger now than in its prime;
A life-line, certain to serve us both a lifetime.

21st December 2016

WHEN YOU ARE GONE

When you are gone
It will be like the setting of the sun.
Time will stand still
And the days will be empty
And difficult to fill.
The heart strings, like cat gut, will be cut.
No love songs to play,
Only memories of melodies
And chords of harmony now passed away.

When you are gone
My world will be shattered like a broken vase.
Sounds will be silent
And sights will be blurred.
The tears will well up
And choke in my throat, gripped in grief.
Little things forgotten,
Brought to mind, remembered;
Sentiments of pity, pain and passion, once begotten.

When you are gone
Your kindness and consideration will be lost.
The sure protection
Which you freely gave
Will remain a debt
Impossible to repay this side of death.
Did you ever know
When your eyes kissed mine
How little time we had before you had to go?

When you are gone
I shall miss your quiet words and ways;
Your inner peace
Which gave me confidence;
Your tender touch
Which cared and calmed my troubled breast.
Your love will live on,
Like the warmth of the sun,
In me and mine, when you are gone.

1974

ALONE, REFLECTING IN THE SUN

If you could only be with me this moment and the more
To share this peaceful hour but for a little while.
To stop and rest and think; it is worthwhile.
To reflect, to recollect, and then to pass a smile....
Some things well remembered and others best forgot:
The things we ought to do, the things we ought not.
To think a little time of nature and of life,
And the reason and the purpose we participate in strife.
Each day we live to encounter good and bad;
Some things make us happy and others make us sad.
Is this for nought, or is there sense in all?
Is there an end, and does man live to fall?
Each individual, born to make the choice between
Belief, or disbelief, as it may seem
To him or her who thinks of these and other things,
From whence our hearts be heavy or may sing.
And when we die, what then; are we but waste?
All knowledge stored in life to rot in but a buried place?
No use, no aim, no after-death, no life to come?
We are alive this peaceful hour,
Alone, reflecting in the sun.

August/September 1959

QUESTIONS ABOUT LIFE

If there was no creation
Why do we create?

If there was no purpose
Why do we act with purpose?

If there was no reason
Why do we have reasons?

If there was no plan
Why do we make plans?

If there was no intelligence
Why do we use intelligence?

If nothing has value
Why do we worship?

If there was no image
Why do we imagine?

If there was no right or wrong
Why do we have conscience?

If there was no God
Why do we try to act like gods?

If there was no perfection
Why do we seek to be perfect?

If there was no salvation
Why do we have faith, hope and love?

If there was no after-life
Why do we go on hoping?

If there was no beginning
Why should there be an end?

If there was ever nothing
Why is there anything?

If life was an accident
Why isn't everything accidental?

If there was no choice
Why do we have freedom?

If there were no answers
Why are there so many questions?

13th December 1974

A LESSON

"Line up properly.
Right
Girls first,
In you go.
Right boys,
Follow on.
Stand up straight everyone,
That includes you, Smith.
Sit down
Quietly!
Take out your books.
Anyone not got a pen?
You'll need your rulers.
I want you to write what's on the board,
Copy it down
Neatly into your books.
Leave a margin.
Don't forget to underline
The heading and the date.
Today, as you can see
We are going to do
'FREEDOM'.
Keep your work tidy.
Remember what I said.
What's the matter, Smith?
No pen?
For God's sake lad,
Why do you always have to be different?
Here, use this one...
Now what's the matter Smith?
No ruler?
God give me strength!

Who hasn't finished yet?
Right. Good.
All, except you Smith.
Hurry up boy,
We can't wait all day for you.

Everyone finished.
At last!
Now, who can define freedom for me?
Doing what you want?
Well, yes, up to a point.
Can anybody add anything to that?
Yes Smith?
What do you mean,
There is no such thing?

Let me explain -
Yes, I know that's the bell.
The bell is for me, not you.
Now where were we?
Oh well,
There isn't time to explain now.
Put your things away.
We'll carry on from here
Next week."

1976

SCHOOL

A place of learning
Canned knowledge
Stuffed down your throat
Only to be spewed up
For exams, and then forgotten.

A place of disciplining
The mind and body,
Having rules without the rod,
Where you can play up
And get out of anything.

A place of working
With irrelevant facts
And pointless information,
Killing interest and
Promoting boredom and ignorance.

A place of teaching
The end, not the beginning,
Of learning about
The unexplored boundaries
Of the world and oneself.

A place of thinking,
Where you are conditioned
To give the right answers
To all the wrong questions
About why you go to school.

May 1975

GETTING NOWHERE

stop.
full   I

a   feel

to   I

come   am

I   going

time   round

each   in
circles

1973

TEACHER

There was a teacher whose only concern
Was the number of passes his pupils could earn.
His reputation
Was their education,
But none of them learnt to love to learn.

1972

EDUCATION

Parents in the land
Tell their kids to give a hand,
Get up, get out and earn some dough,
What do you think your education's for?
We want to get on, and you should too;
Get up, get out and join the queue,
Join the rat race, get what you can,
Twist and steal and dodge the man.
Rent man, tally-man, papers to pay,
All by credit, day to day.
Everybody's doing it, all the nation:
Get what you can with education.

Teachers in the schools,
Teach their pupils all the rules.
Learn this, pass that, like ABC
Don't you know your education's free?
Swot all the facts to learn and learn,
Then one day you'll be able to earn,
Lots of money to spend and spend;
Money can buy you many a friend.
Keep on going from day to day,
Work hard, work fast, no time to play.
All the kids throughout the nation,
Get a good job with education.

Yobs and dropouts all,
Gather round my little stall.
Drugs and pills I have to sell,
Can't you see your education's hell?
Drives you mad with all the chore,
No social life, no life at all - it's all a bore.
Mum's at Bingo, Dad's not here -
Watching telly with a glass of beer.
No time to think, no time to pray,
God forgive us day to day:
All the people in all the nation,
Think again on education.

1965

TOWARDS A JUST SOCIETY

No law can change the hearts of men
Nor put the world to rights;
Just educators know not when
Their pupils see the light.

Where unequal opportunities
And discouragements are rife,
We need a fairer share of inequalities
To supply just "tickets" for life.

February 1987

GLASS DOORS

Shamans, medicine men, witch doctors,
Prophets, priests and seers
Sought to impose order and system
On the scattered arrays of chance,
Interpreting their meanings by ritual and dance.

Oracles and soothsayers,
Guardians of the supernatural,
Passed on their secrets of divination
To the chosen few who were their protégés,
Thus retaining status and honourable patronage.

Now powerless to lock their doors,
The keys to which they hold no more,
Augury's realm of secrecy is smashed
By knowledge winged in the shape of glass,
Cut by reason on a distant shore.
Accessible via the Internet,
Such powers are open to all.

1993

SCHOOL CAT

She walks like a cat, aloof and sleek,
Seemingly soft, cuddly and vulnerable.
Her sharp eyes alert, catching every move;
Timid, but wearing a face of stone.
This girl, in regulation blue, pads to school;
Shabby tiger, alley cat,
Carrying books beneath her arm, she purrs,
Warmed by thoughts of sensuous knowledge.
She comes for cupboard love, not to learn;
Attention, like milk, she laps up with hungry tongue;
She comes to take and not to give,
This earthy creature on the prowl for Tom.
At her desk she sits like Vesta in the hearth,
Body outstretched in lazy recline,
Waiting, watching over her domain,
Ready to pounce or snarl with arrogance
At some unsuspecting innocent who may disturb her peace.
This pampered pet with hidden claws of iron
Could tear out your heart
And watch the tears fall down your face,
Unmoved.

1971

BLUEBELLS

Oh bluebells, you're so beautiful,
Your abundance irrefutable.
My baby daughter
Treats you like water
And wades in, shouting
"Bluetiful!"

1974

LITTLE CHILDREN

Children live in a fantasy world
Of red-eyed monsters
Which come and eat them up
In the night;
Of good fairies
Who collect extracted teeth
And leave some money behind.

Children play at Shops, Doctors and Nurses,
And Mummies and Daddies;
Imitating and reliving experiences
They have known
Or have seen.
They live in a world of adventure
Copying all that they find.

Children live in fear of the dark
Without knowing why;
Of shapes and shadows cast
Upon the wall;
Of strange noises,
Exaggerated by the silence,
Heard in the middle of the night.

Children live in a world of make-believe,
Where everything wrong
Can be made to be right;
Where wishes
All come true.
They pretend to be people they are not
And dress up to suit the occasion.

Children accept what they are taught
Without question;
And are so conditioned by
Mummy and Daddy
And Teacher at school
(Who are fountains of truth to them)
To believe that adults are always right.

Children think that real people are not bad
And that all life is good.
Only witches, ghosts and dragons
Can do evil.
Yet they can be
Cruel to each other without caring,
And ignorant of how and why.

Children love their pets of all kinds,
From horses to dogs.
They love colours and sounds.
They believe in Jesus,
God and Father Christmas
Like little angels, who when it suits,
Can become little devils.

Children take the world for granted
As if it all belongs to them.
As they grow older the dreams
Begin to fade.
They see it as it really is
And are disillusioned by its imperfections,
Wishing all their childhood dreams had been real.

2nd February 1975

PARENTS' "DELIGHT"

There was a young cannibal called Gus
Who used to eat lettuce and stuff
His parents said, "Son,
It's bad for your tum!
Why don't you eat humans like us?"

Gus thought for a time and made up his mind,
One had to be cruel to be kind.
"I'll do as you say
And eat meat from today"
Then he slew them both from behind.

1970

A DAUGHTER'S FRIGHT

Warm and cosy, curled up in bed
She woke with a start and turned her head.
The bedroom door creaked slowly ajar,
A ghostly shadow crawled up the wall.
Cold fear shivered all down her spine
As she suppressed a plaintive whine.
Had a bogeyman come to call
Or a burglar to steal her toys?
She froze and stared wide-eyed in fright
When suddenly all was bathed in light.
It wasn't a phantom or a spectre out to spook,
Only Daddy looking for his puzzle book.

1977

FLOWERS OF YOUTH

Flowers of youth in our good land
Rise up and catch the morning sun.
Gently fold it in your hands,
Keep it with you and have fun,
Take it before the evening comes.

Flowers growing in the sunshine
Stand up and kiss the air we breathe.
Sparkle with your budding minds,
Softly open up your leaves.
Caress the sad and lonely breeze.

Gentle flowers of youth begun,
Colour our world as we pass by.
Meadows made for you to run,
While waving to the distant sky
Taking the clouds of tears to dry.

Flowers of youth, be strong and brave,
Face up and slay the common foe.
Knowing love will always save,
Take it with you when you go,
Before the winds of winter blow.

1974

FAME

There once was a tiger named Ezra
Who wanted to look like a zebra.
With paint black and white
He changed overnight
And became *un tigre célèbre.*

11ᵗʰ December 2013

LIMITATIONS

Amanda
The black and white panda
Wants to fly like the magpie.
Up she jumps
And down she thumps,
Then rubs her bumps with a sigh.
"Oh why can't I fly
Like the birds in the sky?
Do you think I'm foolish to try?"

1978

GEORGIE

The people queued and gladly paid,
For Georgie was the best.
They could not understand his ways,
So anger they suppressed.

Poor Georgie kissed the girls and ran
From bed to bed to rest;
And Georgie satisfied his fans,
For Georgie was the best.

The best of Georgie was to come,
For Georgie was the best;
But Georgie felt that he was done
So gave football a rest.

He drank, he gambled, played the bore,
Poor Georgie blamed the press.
He stayed at home, then played abroad,
For Georgie was the best.

He sought a cure to gain some pride
For Georgie was the best.
He took a wife and tried to hide;
And gave the drink a rest.

Alas, he lapsed and beat his wife;
A drunkard at his best.
The surgeons tried to save his life:
George drank himself to death.

He could not cope with all the fame,
For Georgie was the best.
But in the end he made his name
Just being Georgie Best.

1982

SOCCER GIRL

She's a true football fanatic
Everywhere you'll find her at it;
She'll give you a kick if you get in her way,
And boot the poor coach if he won't let her play
Football.

She'll play anywhere to get it,
People say she's 'energetic'.
If you want her to score, just give her the ball,
Then hug her and kiss her and tell her it's called
"Football".

She's the queen of the soccer scene,
Superstar of her local team.
If you shoot her a line, she'll say she is game,
She'll always play ball if you mention the name
"Football".

Everyone thinks that she looks weird;
She's six foot six and sports a beard.
They all get a fright when she comes out to play
And run for their lives when they think it is 'gay'
Football.

She's got FIFA in a whirl,
People call her "Georgie Girl".
She's the best in all the world.
She's appeared on telly with mud on her chest;
She's a female Pele, a Matthews and Best
Of all -
'Cause she's no boob with a ball!

1980

OFFSIDE

A bastard.
Born out of wedlock,
My mother not a wife,
My father not a husband,
No legal rights.
Both too scared to commit,
Too selfish to make me legit.
I feel I want to hide;
It's as if they've scored a goal
And I've been ruled offside.

27th February 2014

TAKE THE SUN

Take the morning sun
And fold it in your hand.
Take it with you when you go,
I'll keep the home fires burning.
You will see the seeds you sow
Growing in the land of learning.
Flower of youth so young
Shine forth out of the desert sand.
Unfold your petals and glow,
Satisfy your curious yearning.
When the heat has gone
And you're strong enough to stand,
You will feel the life-blood flow
With your experience and discerning.
Leaves will fall in autumn
As Nature does demand,
So take the sun and blow,
Before the winter comes in mourning.

1972

TREE SPEECH

The dawn chorus is
A natural alarm clock
Of signs and signals.

The sound messages
Are the battle cries of birds
In choral warfare.

Communication
System with a limited
Vocabulary.

Reports about food,
Boundaries and moods, to mates
Waiting in the wings.

Each species' mating
Call, is a sound barrier
To inter-breeding.

Be not deluded,
Even by the twitter and
Charm of chaffinches.

The birds sing to birds
While we talk to cats, which oft
Regard us as trees.

Spring 1976

WEEPING WILLOW

Morning, afternoon and night,
Here I'm rooted to the spot.
Casting shadows in the light;
Weeping is my chosen lot.

Here I'm rooted to the spot,
In the garden at the front.
Weeping is my chosen lot.
When gales rage I bear the brunt.

In the garden at the front,
My arms reach down to touch the ground.
When gales rage I bear the brunt;
The only time I make a sound.

My arms reach down to touch the ground,
Making real my worldly fears.
The only time I make a sound,
I'm moved to mourn the passing years.

Making real my worldly fears
With every passing friend and foe,
I'm moved to mourn the passing years;
I stand and shed soft tears of woe.

I stand and shed soft tears of woe,
In silence weep sweet tears of joy
With every passing friend and foe,
For each new baby girl and boy.

24th February 1982

30

IN NATURE'S GARDEN

Flowers blossom in the summer sun
Then fade away in the evening shade.
Shadows of their former selves, they droop,
The beauty of their youth betrayed.

In time each bloom will don its splendour
Bestowing colour on our mundane lives.
Scents and hues bombard our senses
Bringing joy to hearts and tears to eyes.

Every flower has its purpose.
Ask the bees that come to call.
When petals fold and day is over,
Remember loved ones when they fall.

13th January 2016

THE FOUR SEASONS

Young lovers strolling hand in hand,
Children playing,
The days stretching longer,
Buds bursting forth,
Rain showers with the sun breaking through.
Shadows becoming stronger,
Lambs gambolling in the fields;
Great patches of greenery unfold
As the clouds roll back
To reveal the spring.

Colours and flowers abound in glory,
Crowds jostling,
Lazing in country fields,
Garden barbecues,
Sunburn lotion and sultry nights.
Salad and fresh fruit for meals,
The stillness of a heat haze,
Sweat running off the brow,
All juices flowing fast,
Rising to salute the summer.

Shrivelled and shrinking, growing old,
Leaves falling,
Nature's back is bent.
The biting wind, howling,
Grey skies and lashing rain
Hustle autumn to retirement.

Paint peeling off the window ledge,
The days, like steps, becoming shorter.
Bodies running out of steam
Cannot keep up the pace.

Ice on the pond, thick fog and frost;
Snowflakes drifting;
A cold, deserted landscape.
Old age creeping;
The living, sleeping-death of hibernation.
Brittle branches break
Like bones on skeleton trees.
First signs of resurrection show;
The robin on the garden gate.
And winter once again recedes
In deference to spring.

14th January 1974

A NEW BEGINNING

We started off as husband and wife.
I believe she was the love of my life,
But slowly she became a sister -
And I really came to miss her.

She cared for me and life was good.
She gave me all the things she could.
She cooked and cleaned and managed by stealth
But less and less she gave herself.

In earlier years the seeds were sown
And for decades apathy had grown,
Then on maturity all seemed lost,
Killed off by middle-aged frost.

I prayed and wooed with all my might
Hoping all would once again come right.
Then, I know not how, I know not when
The seeds of love were sown again:
"I'm totally yours," she sighed one night,
"I'm here for you, so do what you like."

2013

HOPE

Hope is a product of desire
A flame from a passionate fire
Flickering small or licking tall
The walls of kind or mal-intent.
Smouldering ashes, dreams destroyed,
Fanned by fluctuating gusts of wind
Ignite the debris of discontent
Which piled too high consumes within.

Hope has new horizon faces
To lighten the darkest places.
A dawn each day along each way
Alleviates depressing night;
A smile or an encouraging word
From stranger or from passer-by,
A lighthouse beam, a flash of white
On stormy seas of black despair.

Hope is a traveller unpaid.
In time, a servant not a slave:
Cast in a spell in a wishing well;
A footprint in the desert sand;
The sound of laughter far away;
An ambulance, a distress flare.
In times of stress a helping hand
Or a lifebuoy self-inflated.

Hope is a child of want which cries.
When pacified it slowly dies.
Hope has never ending worth,
Borne to give us second birth.

Autumn 1976

35

CHANGE

Life is good,
Full of love;
From above
Comes all we need.
Times are so easy,
We tend to forget.
I wish you'd believe me,
You'd have no regrets.

If you stay
You will pay
For the day
When all is gone.
Don't be so dreamy,
You don't have to yawn.
Change is so easy,
Wake up to the dawn.

Like I said,
You'll see red
If you're dead
When all arise.
Don't be so greedy
With money and power.
You may not believe me,
But now is the hour.

You must change,
Or be changed.
Cut those chains
From off your feet.
Who is the master,
Who is the man,
We follow after,
As best we can?

1974

WHO IS LIKE THE LORD?

Muslims, Christians, Jews,
Monotheists everywhere,
Call me Yahweh, Allah, God
Yet drive me to despair.
We are all the same,
No need to choose -
But if I were your Creator
I would tell you now, not later,
That fighting over who is right or wrong
Is wrong and wrong, so wrong.
What kind of deity am I
Who lets you live with blinkered eye?
I did not create so you could kill.
You have misunderstood my will.
You are meant to love instead of hate.

Therein lies *your* ultimate fate.
Wise up and put your arms away
And fill the world with peace today.
If you *really* want to worship me,
Then learn to live in harmony.

27th September 2014

MAN ON THE CROSS

Long, long ago, a carpenter's son
Cut all his ties with his home and was gone,
Wandering around in the heat of the sun
Carving his name on the hearts he turned on.

He questioned his elders and punctured their pride.
Their power and position he chopped down to size.
They waited to bait him, to trap him they tried,
But none could avoid the look in his eyes.

His friends were the poor and deprived of his day,
The outcasts and driftwood of death and decay.
He helped them to burn all their props and to say
"This is the life" and "This is the way".

He loosened the chains for all men to be free.
Their hang-ups he hung on that Calvary tree.
They crowned him with thorns and mocked him with glee.
"Betrayed by a kiss, king of love, come and see!"

"Oh why were you dying, man on the cross?
Why were you crying, *'lama sabachthani'*?
Who could abide that man on the cross?
The blood from the nails in his flesh flowed for us.

*'lama sabachthani' means 'why have you forsaken me?' in
Aramaic, the language Jesus spoke.

11ᵗʰ January 1975

I'LL DO ANYTHING

Throw me a rubber and I'll rub out my name.
Give me a gun and I'll blow out my brains.
Show me the sun and I'll hold back the rain.
Love me today and I'll love you the same.
Leave me tomorrow and I'd die from the pain.
Do what you like, I'll take all the blame.
Deceive me, desert me, I'll cover your shame.
Reject me, forsake me, I'll forgive you again.
Ignore me, forget me, my love will remain.

1970

FRIENDS

Friends are people who will give their lives for you,
The rest are but acquaintances.
Friends are more precious than gold or silver
And just as hard to find.
Friends are more beautiful than diamonds or pearls;
Their love never fades in the darkest moments.
Friends are like rare and delicate plants
Which, when found, need tender care.
Friends are more reliable than modern computers;
They give you the truth without your asking.
Friends are free and cannot be bought;
They give and do not look for any reward.
Friends will share their lives with you forever,
If you can lose yourself in theirs.
To lose a friend is to lose a little of yourself
And the world is poorer by the loss.
To find a friend helps you find yourself,
For friends make life worth living.

8th December 1974

COLOUR BLIND IN '59

A member of our Commonwealth
A Britisher like me
Arrived in England.
He tried to find a house or flat,
Somewhere to stay
But the problem was his colour,
It was black.

We advocate equality,
We teach it in our schools.
Equality for all.
Some people slammed their doors at that,
No room for more.
The problem was his colour,
It was black.

At last he found a place to live,
The landlord called it 'home'.
A tiny room.
The walls were soaking front and back,
But never mind,
You paid a little extra
Being black.

He found a job to pay his way.
His education sound,
His word his bond.
There was nothing that this man did lack
Except one thing,
For when it came to colour
He was black.

The white man had his pride to keep,
The black man had the same
But not his freedom.
The neighbours never called him "Jack"
They called him "Coon".
The reason was his colour,
It was black.

God made the races, four in all:
Pink, yellow, red and brown,
Bestowed with love.
He blessed them all, the world to pack
With mortal souls.
There are no colours
White or black,
So racists, you've been told.

1964

RICKY

My canine friend came from the vet.
We took him in without regret.
Alsatian-Collie cross was he;
A friendly dog we called 'Ricky'.

He licked my hands when we first met
And toured the garden in the wet,
Deciding that his home was set.
I swore to him he'd always be
                My canine friend.

Whenever left, he'd sit and fret
But proved a very faithful pet.
I took him walks in pastures free;
Their streams he used to jump with me.
I doubt if ever I'll forget
                My canine friend.

20ᵗʰ February 1982

MICKEY THE MONKEY

Mickey the Monkey
Lives in a tree.
He knows his numbers,
One, two, three.

One for the monkey
Two for the tree.
Three for the letters
ABC.

Mickey the Monkey
Looks down on me.
He walked with angels
Out of the sea.

A is for ape-man
B is for me.
C is for cloning
One, two, three.

Mickey the Monkey
Can talk to me.
He told me the secret
Of Sirius B.

Was it a spaceman
Up in the tree?
Whence came the monkey
Came you and me?

1981

BEAUTY AND THE BEAST

"You're a beauty," said he.
"And so are you," the Beauty said.
"No I'm not, I'm ugly" said he.
"Then so am I," the Beauty said.

"I love beauty," he said.
"And I love you," said the Beauty.
"Oh, it's not you I love, but your beauty," he said.
"Oh, you beast!" said she.

1975

TRUE LOVE?

He said he loved her
But he left her wild
When she told him
She was having his child.
She told her parents,
They told her to go:
"Go live with your lover,
We don't want to know".

The neighbours judged her,
Said she was a tart.
No ring on her finger,
No hope in her heart.
She went on her way
To live all alone,
No friends or relations
Offered a home.

Now she is a mother
And cares for her son.
She feeds and she clothes him
And they live as one.
No hope to be married,
Her purity stained;
Few men want a woman
Who's second-hand gained.

Take care with the 'letters'
For words can come cheap.
If actions speak louder,
Beware what they reap.

Should sins of the spirit
Be worse than the flesh,
Forgive all our lusting,
May true love be blessed.

1970

LOVE

Love is more than kinship,
Love is more than companionship.
Love is growing togetherness,
Love is knowing madness;
Love is in the mind,
Love is blind.

Love is more than lusting,
Love is more than trusting,
Love is meeting needs.
Love is shown in deeds;
Love is in the giving,
Love is living.

Love is more than demanding,
Love is more than understanding,
Love is needing each other;
Love is being another.
Love is in the sharing,
Love is caring,

Love is.

9th February 1975

47

CARE

It is too easy to say we care
From the comfort of an armchair.
Anyone can "care about",
Even the most common lout.
At a distance conscience pangs
Are smothered by more urgent plans.
It is a lie to say we care
When we are not actually there.
Loving activates the will to do
Whatever caring must be done.
It costs us time and effort too -
Committed "caring for" someone.

8th May 1996

DUTY BOUND

No worse love than duty;
To care for
But not adore,
To look after
Without laughter,
To give
And not live.
The receiver
Is not the deceiver.
"Duty Bound"
Makes a hollow sound;
Even to those who are well
It can seem an emotional hell.

September 2013

ACTIONS SPEAK

Love and care are more oft caught
Than by some formal lesson taught.
Where principle and practice meet
The paradigm makes life more sweet.

12th January 2013

AWAY WITH WORDS

Restless hands entwined,
Thumbs touching palms
Pushing buttons, stirring desire.
Your knowing looks and comic glare,
Those captive eyes which mesmerised,
Causing heads to turn and stare.
Warm hands cupping my unsure face
Focusing my attention.
Soft fingers gently ploughing through my hair
Slowly smoothing away all cares,
Creating furrows straight and true
Sweeping worries from the air.
A waft of breath upon my neck
When cuddled up against the cold.
A familiar tap on wrist or arm,
The times you stroked my inner thigh,
Stoking lust to further highs.
Signs and signals, thoughts untold,
All these and more I miss,
With no last chance to say "Goodbye"
Nor seal our loving with a kiss,
No words can tell.

13ᵗʰ December 2013

CAN YOU NOT HEAR MY WORDS?

Your beauty blinds me like the blazing sun,
I cannot look you in the face;
I stand mouth opened wide, struck dumb.
Can you not hear my words?
Is this the time and place?

Whispered greetings, dispersed in confined spaces,
I want to speak and tell you all,
But mute I am for fear of my disclosure.
Can you not hear my words?
Can you not hear my call?

Temptations play upon my mind.
I wait for you to care.
My passion, frightening to behold, is blind.
Can you not hear my words?
Consumed with lust, beware!

My heart and mind are torn in two.
To hold your hand is all I ask.
Such emptiness of soul, I never knew.
Can you not hear my words?
Hold on, I will complete the task!

We meet from time to time, a fleeting glance.
Do I detect in you the same emotions
Flowing through you in some ritualistic dance?
Can you not hear my words?
Come listen to my sweet devotions.

Silent as the night and deep in thought,
I wonder if you really know;
My secret hopes remain at nought.
Can you not hear my words?
Love takes a time to grow.

Gentle is the breeze and softly falls the snow.
I kneel upon the ground in silent prayer
Offering thanks, at last you know;
You've heard my silent words
And now I know you care.

June 1968

TYPING

Typing is writing
Mechanical fashion
Letters in fetters
Released by the hand.
Notions in motion
Float across keyboard
Passing from mind
Into matter in bands.
Ribbon well hidden
Printing black words,
Posted to people
In far-away lands.
Carriage release
And carriage return,
Round paper bail
Shifting its stand.
Rivers of figures
Flooding the page
Ripple the surface
Channelled by man.
Typing, like writing,
Is tiring and testing
As hard on the hands
As scouring black pans.

January 1977

IT'S A BORING ROUTINE

It's a boring routine
Getting dirty things clean.
Every day it's the same
Till my lover comes home again.

Monday morning,
Get up in plenty of time,
Get the kids off to school
In a bit of a rush.
Got to get the washing out
On the line.

Gather the clothes,
Hoping the weather stays fine.
Do the shopping in town
In a bit of a rush.
Got to get the washing out
On the line.

Washing machine
Hums and gives me the sign.
Throw in the dirty old clothes
In a bit of a rush.
Got to get the washing out
On the line.

Into the dryer
Which spins and makes a whine.
Take a trip out the back
In a bit of a rush.
Got to get the washing out
On the line.

Monday evening
My lover comes home on time.
Get the kids off to bed
In a bit of a rush.
Then bring the washing in
Off that line.

It's a boring routine;
Well you know what I mean!
Every night it's the same
When my lover comes home again.

1973

WHEN YOU ARE BORED

When you are bored
Let time stand still and think a while
Of me and of love stored
In these few words, which with a smile
You may reflect upon and know
That I am with you when you're bored.
Let time pass by and fill your mind
With thoughts of love sweet absence finds;
For love is life and life renewed.
Remember this when you are bored
With nothing else to do but brood;
For I am with you, love restored,
Till time betwixt us is no more,
And here I sit, right by your side,
For love, it knows no law.
And so as always I abide,
In thought and word, with you,
This moment... when you're bored.

1960

TIME

Time is what we call it by any other name:
Seconds could be minutes,
Hours could be days,
Weeks could be months
And years could be seconds.
Time is, was, and ever shall be
Without beginning, without end;
A cycle of tomorrows,
Todays and yesterdays.
The future becomes the present
Which becomes the past.
Time is first and last.
We make it our servant
But serve as its slave.
We live hand in hand with it
Until we reach the grave;
Then we are left behind
While time marches on,
Relentlessly.

24ᵗʰ December 1974

TIME AND TIDE

At an ebbing three score years and ten
I have become a man of easy tears.
My approaching death, not if but when,
Makes me mourn the loss of future years.
My loved ones may miss me more than I them,
For I shall have shed all human fears,
No longer swayed by the tides of men.

31st October 2012

THE FISHERMEN OF CALDEY

We went to see the dropouts
On the Isle of Caldey.
Some of them were holy
And others had simply
Dropped in for the day.

We went by boat from Tenby
The "fishermen" to see.
While some caught dabs at sea
Others were on dry land,
Odd-men-out making scent.

We landed at the slipway
And spied a sign for shortbread.
Some people went well-fed,
Food provided daily,
While other people starved.

57

We entered the island shop,
Packed full of souvenirs
And gifts to ward off fears.
Perfume sold like hot cakes;
A brand new 'Bread of Life'.

The Christians were all trading
Selling their wares for cash.
The House of God can't last
Coining money like a mint,
As in the Temple yard.

We visited the lighthouse.
The keepers all were gone.
No shining light was on.
No one to show the way.
The monks were all at prayer.

I entered the monastery
Seeking spiritual life.
I couldn't take my wife;
Women were excluded.
I felt that way within.

The monks take vows of silence,
Obedience and chastity;
A cloistered fraternity
With masochistic needs
Hidden behind closed doors.

We left the Isle of Caldey,
Our pilgrimage was done.
Refreshment, we found none.
Where were those "fishermen",
Not catching fish but men
Who served the Holy One?

August 1975

A BALLADE OF THE SEA

Paragon of power, the pundits say,
Your breathing causes waves to rise and fall.
Bathers run to greet you, shouting "Hurray!"
But your swift embrace can become a maul
And the kiss of death awaits one and all.
Your beauty is deceptive; blue is grey.
Standard colours of tyrants always pall;
You will not have your way with me today.

Tempestuous lover enticing and gay,
Luring your victims from behind your shawl,
Leading both young and old alike astray.
There are suckers at every market stall
And you, old-timer with your loathsome gall
Give licence to travel and right of way
To any who ask it, great and small.
You will not have your way with me today.

There is nothing for which we do not pay.
You foam at the mouth when angry in squall
And your frothy tongue licks round every bay.
Hard rugged rocks and coastlines form a wall,
Hence to be washed away, however tall.
Ships, homes, lives of people at work or play.
But I am not to be part of your haul,
You will not have your way with me today.

Envoi

Sea, I can hear your terrible hunger call;
The rumblings in your belly as you sway.
Yes, even I can touch you when you crawl.
You will not have your way with me today.

August 1976

60

A SHIP DIES

A ship, a wreck upon the heavy seas
Floats helpless, empty, all alone.
Buffeted by mountainous waves, it reels
From side to side, heading for home.

The wind whistles round the mast
And clouds of spray fly past the bridge.
Her sides are gashed, she's sinking fast;
This ship, iced-up like a giant fridge.

The Arctic waters, grey with gloom,
Rise and fall in rhythmic motion,
Beating out a warning of impending doom.
The ship, still flooding, lies lower in the ocean.

The icebergs, like an angry mob, hold back,
Watching as their victim slowly dies.
The ship, abandoned, lonely, painted black,
Smoothly slides beneath the waves without a sigh.

1973

AT SEAHOUSES

Seahouses, grey and so damp did seem
And dark were the islands of Farne.
The waves lay calm but the seagulls screamed
And still was the air with alarm.

The morning mist o'er the sea did rise
And pale shone the watery sun.
The time had come for the seals to die
And cold were the hearts of our young.

The fishermen in their boats stood proud
But sad were the eyes of my son.
Policemen came to control the crowds
Who cried that the deed be not done.

Then the marksmen with their guns held tight
Went out on the ebb of the tide.
Their shots rang out and the seals took fright,
For them there was no place to hide.

Three thousand seals, grey and white, lay dead
And gone was their watery calm.
Their blood flowed quick and the sea turned red
And black were the clouds over Farne.

Easter 1975

VIEWS AROUND KYNANCE

Westward on the distant horizon line
Rests Penwith, now glass-clear, now smudged in haze;
A granite peninsula, dark, remote,
Like a watching finger marking time.
Across Mounts Bay flash red and white rays;
The eyes of Wolf Rock searching out boats
Around Land's End, down a coast of serpentine.

Behold! Kynance, showplace of the Lizard,
With its manifold elaborations;
The Gull Rock and Asparagus Island;
Black rocks colour-washed like witch and wizard;
A cove, steeple pierced with incantations,
Rainbows of spray above floss-silk sand.
Its beauty fretted by winter blizzards.

Behind, bulked large, the headland of the Rill:
A tableland's edge, whence first was sighted
The coming of the Spanish Armada.
Before sits Lion Rock, with looks to kill,
Guarding the cove and cliffs, his mane blighted,
Head turned, watching the sea and its saga
Beneath the ridge of Yellow Carn, quite still.

Inland, to the north, are the war-stained downs,
Where airfields scar and slice both hill and heath.
Predannack, Goonhilly and far Culdrose
With tumuli and furze in stony ground;
Land most holy, enchanted, wild and bleak
Now house a heliport, saucers and roads;
Solitude shed by the droning of sound.

63

East of the Lion, the scarf of Pentreath,
A sweep of sand against fierce cliffs' wall,
Brushed by the foaming surf of man-high waves.
Yet Pentreath is a plain and tranquil beach,
The most romantic and charming of all,
Where adders bask on hot summer days
And men go a-launcing on moonlit trysts.

Below our window, the end of the lawn,
Where cropped grass topples into barley fields
Which slope to the sea to the south and west.
From here we see vessels Atlantic born
And pass away as the sea-sky yields.
Of all panoramas this is the best;
Large ships and small boats parading from dawn.

Southward, the land falls to old Lizard Head
And a vast arc of luminous green sea.
Beyond are The Stags and old Man o' War;
Great stones out of sight, dark reefs for the dead.
Rocks to which only shags and cormorants flee.
A coastguard lookout hut above the shore
Acts as medic to a constant deathbed.

A little below us along the road
Beside Maenheere where a tricolour waved,
On the first morning of Armistice Day,
A Belgian widow and daughter abode
The husband drowned, but his parrot was saved;
Some say the shock made the parrot turn grey.
What happened to them is no longer told.

Down farther yet to narrow Rocky Lane,
Sunk between bramble, boulder and high fern;
And on, beside squelching trickle of stream
To Pistol Meadow, of mounded square fame,
Where two hundred souls, from legend we learn,
Were washed ashore and then buried in seams;
Men of war felled by the Rock of that name.

It is said hordes of dogs raced to the scene
To eat the bodies cast up from the wreck.
Hundreds of firearms and cannon were found
But wreckers soon came to pick the place clean.
Don't go at night if you value your neck.
It is haunted and eerie, odd without sound,
And many strange sights are said to be seen.

Cross over the stream where tamarisks hang.
Step up the steep weedy stairs to the cliff
Which leads to the least troubled Lizard cove.
Behind us the seaweed camomile tang.
Ahead, the old lifeboat station and slip,
Polpeor, where Tennyson bathed, I'm told,
And on to the southernmost point of land.

About us, a chain of bright brimming pools,
The spatter of pebbles and sand on shore,
The incessant wash and drag of the tide,
A natural arch, a cavern for fools.
Gullies, clefts, coves, caves and rock-falls galore;
A coastline dragon-green monster waves ride
Breathing white fire, crested with silver, they rule.

Eastward, the lighthouse lime-washed dazzling white,
Directs the liners, oil tankers and boats
Away from the booming cannon-fired sea.
Its beam like a tongue, licks the skyline night,
Silently warning anything afloat
Of treachery beneath, on bended knee;
The beam like a sword at the Old Head swipes.

Return along lanes meandering back
Past Penmenner House, now only a wraith,
Down an arras of fuchsia draping stone,
Where wallflowers roof the rough gravel track
Beyond feathered plumes of tamarisk waifs
To the house "Kynance Bay", once Trewin's home.
Such envious views the rest of Cornwall lacks.

August 1976

MY LOVELY MAIDEN

She was my lovely maiden
Whose eyes were bright as pearls.
She was my lovely maiden
Who loved the deep blue sea,
But now she is in heaven,
A place I'll never be.
She was my lovely maiden
And she was good for me.

My heart is heavy laden,
My eyes they smart with tears.
My heart is heavy laden
Now she has gone from me.
She didn't mind the weather
And she was lost at sea.
My heart is heavy laden,
Our love now cannot be.

We tried to find a haven,
Our hearts were filled with fear.
We tried to find a haven,
Her end it was to be;
For we sailed away together
But waves swept her from me.
We tried to find a haven,
Her haven was the sea.

1976

MY GEORDIE LADDIE

I went with my Geordie laddie
For a neet oot on the toon.
We had a dance, we had a laugh
We had some Fed and Broon.
Alas the beor was too strong
And he kept falling doon.
My laddie to a netty went
Then said "Ah'll see yes soon".

I went with my Geordie laddie
To St. James's Park one day.
He said it wor a reet good treat
To watch the Magpies play.
Alas the team were all at sea
And threw the game away.
My laddie, he was sore upset
And said he couldna stay.

I went with my Geordie laddie
To the Sunday Market quay.
We stood beside the River Tyne,
He said we'd married be.
Alas, I saw it was nay good,
His heart cried to be free.
I told him so and he got mad
And said he'd go to sea.

I went with my Geordie laddie
To Jesmond Dene today.
We sat beside the waterfall,
The sky came over grey.
Alas, a da' he was to be;
I found it hard to say.
My laddie said he had nay job
And so he couldna pay.

I went with my Geordie laddie
To his home in Benwell Grove.
He there did vow to spill his blood
But said his seed should grow.
Alas, the Tyne Bridge was the place
And there we had to go.
He planned to jump and end his life -
Then said it wasn't so!

I said to my Geordie laddie
As he walked away from me
"Weor ya gannin hinney?"
And he replied, as if surprised,
"Aam gannin heam hinney!"
I coulda cried.

1975

AT LYME REGIS

As we strolled along the promenade at Lyme
We watched the raging sea below.
We felt the waves of passion rise and fall
Knowing our time would ebb and flow.

The stars like windows slowly hidden
By curtains of cloud, silent drawn
Across the sky by some invisible hand,
Kept us apart as we tried to keep warm.

As we looked out across the bay
The lighthouse flashed its warning light.
We kept our distance like the ships at sea,
Taking care to sail a course we knew was right.

We played with ideas to breach the gap
As we ambled side by side, not touching.
Giddy words danced across our lips
And we laughed at silly pointless things.

Our thoughts were in turmoil like the waters below
And our minds cut off from those around;
Like pebbles thrown up in a mass of spray
We hoped there was a haven to be found.

Did we think we could survive like the dinosaurs?
Would we stand together and never suffer loss?
Hand in hand and cheek to cheek, we faced the open sea.
Come the day of reckoning, could we ever count the cost?

As we peered into the harbour from the Cobb,
The deep black water lapped along the wall.
Did you sense the heartbeat racing in my breast?
Did you hear my stifled, anguished mating call?

Can you share the depths of my emotions?
Are your moods in harmony with mine?
When I touch you, do you tremble?
Can you walk the pathways of my mind?

As we made our way back to the car on foot
Retracing steps we'd taken earlier on,
We shared the moment of a lifetime
Wondering whether we should carry on.

11th February 1974

THE STORY OF THE DINOSAURS

Before the orogenesis
Of the Alps and Andes;
Before the Himalayas,
Rockies and Pyrenees
Folded into the blue sky;
Before Man had his birth
And wrote his name in the sand,
Dinosaurs ruled the Earth.

The Book of Earth History
Four thousand six hundred
Pages, a million years long,
Leaves a lot to be read.
The dinosaurs fill some
One hundred and thirty
While mere Man appears
On the last page only.

Humans never saw their success
Nor witnessed the decline
Of these lords of creation.
 In their Triassic prime
They straddled the shrinking globe
In majestic splendour,
Dominating continents,
Paragons of power.

Elite of the Reptile Age,
With egg-brains at their core,
Two-footed and four-footed
Carnivores and herbivores;
Horned, spiked, long-necked, duck-billed,
Large, medium and small.
Some monsters walked upright.
Some crawled on all fours.

The Mesozoic era
Of prehistoric beasts,
Gave pride of place to tyrants
In tropical world heat.
Terrible lizards roaming
Upland, swamp and jungle;
Swimmers, diggers, tree-climbers,
Tearing Earth asunder.

A two-legged meat eater,
Awful Allosaurus,
Swept Jurassic landscapes
Hunting Brontosaurus.
Theropod of theropods,
Tyrannosaurus Rex,
King killer of Cretaceous,
A cannibal, came next.

Sounds of brawn reverberant
Rumbled beneath the ground,
Like distant thunder coming
When these giants roamed around;
Cold-blooded automatons
Who killed without a care.
The modern bear and lion
Are harmless dwarfs, compared.

T.Rex, with mouth a metre wide,
Armed with scimitar-teeth
And hands hooked with tearing claws,
Was truly a masterpiece:
The ultimate in brute strength,
A tale of brawn triumphant
Over brain for generations,
Till victor lay defunct.

(Dinosaurs, oh dinosaurs,
Oh why are you extinct?
Was it racial senescence
Or did you never think?
Chromosomes in chaos
Producing toothless freaks?
Who preyed upon your eggs
And relatives did eat?
Did the climate grow too cold?
Were there epidemics?
Did your food supply all fold?
Were changes far too quick?)

Evolution has its failures.
The dinosaur was one.
Compared to the dinosaurs
Man is but Tom Thumb.
Should we ever be their peers
We need to survive
Another one hundred
And twenty-nine million years.

1977

AN ISLAND EXPERIENCE

There was a time when passion made my stomach
Do a somersault;
When aching limbs and throbbing heart
Made fire within my soul.
But now the ticks of time have slowed me down
And worn away the fuse to blow me up inside;
So now I know that I am growing old.
The uncertainty of youth
Which once could cause distress
Has grown to be a steady anchor in the waters
Of my decaying prime.
Like a boat long-moored, which breaks up and rots,
Its timbers floating on a wearing sea no tide can stop,
I'm helpless, but at one with time.

That sure-footed arrogance peculiar to youth
Which helped me climb the highest cliffs
Whose rocks were thousands of millions of times
Older than myself;
Which made me think I could compete with Nature
And succeed;
To conquer all, I understand,
Was just an ego-tripping cry for help,
Desperate to prove myself a man.

The rocks and sea will still be here when I am gone.
Now I must learn to crawl back to the sea.
No further hope of being washed up on the shore.
No wasted dreams to tie me any more,
For I am conquered by the One Who gave me birth.
This island home I must desert
On a one-way trip, never to return
I kiss the rocks goodbye.

18th April 1972

HEADS AND TALES

The wide oceans,
The high mountains,
The trees in the woods,
Have stories to tell —
If only they could.

The leaves on the trees,
The fish in the sea,
The birds in the sky,
Have tales to tell —
If only they'd try.

The rocks on land,
The desert sand,
The flowers in bud,
Have stories to tell —
If only they would.

Clouds in the air,
Waves on the water,
Spray in the wind,
Sweep over my head
Telling their tales
In a howling gale.

1977

STORM IN A TEACUP?

Cumulus clouds accumulate
When water droplets form
Heated by the burning earth
Brewing up a thunderstorm.

From drought to flood and round again
Such crises loom and leave;
And people pour their troubles out
By brewing cups of tea.

28th July 2013

78

CLOUDS

Clouds,
Shifting, drifting,
On cushions of air, floating
Round a fantasy world
In a Freudian head
Well-hidden.

Clouds,
Moving, soothing,
Great vapours of mist, cooling
Shapeless amoebic masses
Changing abstract patterns,
On a blue sky.

Clouds,
Heavy, earthbound,
In depressing cells, falling
Down damp decaying walls,
As monotonous drips
I reach out to touch.

1977

HEAVY SHOWER

Footsteps splattered like wet fish
On the stone pavements of the streets.
People hunched and huddled,
Darted for refuge from the sheeting rain.

I nestled in a doorway
Mesmerised by the rhythmic beat:
Pit-a-pat, pit-pat – plop,
Drips dropped from the gutters overhead.

My skin bristled up in waves
As I lolled snug in a doorway.
The water gurgled down drains
And gushed spluttering from the pipes.

The neon amber street lights
Cast a warm glow on the buildings.
Walls and roof-tops gleamed brightly.
A new-look, fresh sheen, bestowed on everything.

As the downfall subsided,
And floodwater ran off in streams
Fast disappearing underground,
I felt a slow wet trickle down my neck.

22ⁿᵈ January 1975

WHERE WERE YOU?

Where were you when I sought you
Down the darkened lanes at night
And chased your shadow
Up blind alleys?
Were you ever there?
And when I wandered the streets
In hope of meeting you,
Did I really ever see you?
How will I ever know
If what I saw was true?
And when I thought I caught
A fleeting glimpse of you
Among the crowds,
I danced and dodged and bobbed
My way to where you stood.
You were not there;
I found another standing in your place.
Where did you go?
Did you know,
And run to hide your face?
Did you laugh when you saw my tears?
And when I strolled by your house,
Did I see you sitting at your window
Waiting for a sight of me?
Or were you simply there by chance?
And when I cast my eye
In your direction,
Did you want to see me
On the outside looking in?
If I'd stopped and knocked upon your door
Would you have welcomed me within?

1969

81

THE KNOCK UPON YOUR DOOR

As you sit and ponder in your
Semi-detached suburban home,
Do you ever wonder why
You live at all?

Washing the dishes, cleaning the floor,
Darning and mending,
Do you stop
To answer the knock upon your door?

As you relax in your favourite chair,
Head back and cool,
Do you ever wonder why
You live at all?

Watching the telly, reading a book,
Hoping and praying,
Do you rise
To answer the knock upon your door?

As you take off your clothes
And prepare for bed,
Do you ever wonder why
You live at all?

Making a meal, checking your change,
Scrimping and saving,
Do you run
To answer the knock upon your door?

As you lie awake beneath the sheets,
Your body limp,
Do you ever wonder why
You live at all?

Feeding your child, wiping the tears,
Caring and tending,
Do you need
To answer the knock upon your door?

As you eat your breakfast
In the early morn
Do you ever wonder why
You live at all?

Cleaning your shoes, leaving the house,
Rushing and cursing:
Do you remember
The sound of knocking on your door?

No one is there.
Your lover, in despair, has gone
And you were the one
Who ignored
His knocking on your door.
His heart is cold
His love is dead.
And you,
Who walk along the street
All dressed to kill,
Do you ever wonder why
You live at all?

1969

WILL YOU REMEMBER?

Will you remember today, my love,
When you are old and grey?
The words we spoke in confidence,
Our secret trysts for conference?
Will you remember today, my love,
When duty caused delay?
Will you remember
Our first embrace?
Will you remember
The time and place?

Will you remember today, my love,
Should you move far away?
Our kiss-shaped cross of empathy,
The times we shared in ecstasy?
Will you remember today, my love
The songs of love I played?
Will you remember
The way we sighed?
Will you remember
The tears we cried?

Will you remember today, my love,
Should you decide to stay?
Obsessive instincts and desires,
Our mutual bondage needs inspire.
Will you remember today, my love,
When conscience calls to pay?
Will you remember
How much we pined?
Will you remember
Our limbs entwined?

Will you remember
To look into my eyes
And not despise today?
For it is over, gone.
Our hearts and minds,
Our bodies, souls,
Are now as one,
My love.

1968

MY DREAM OF LOVE

I love to dream my dream of love
My thoughts my own,
I walk alone
And in my walking wake the sleeping,
Dreaming of my dream of love.

And in my dream I hold no hate,
No anger to suppress.
I talk no less
And in my talking wake the dreaming,
Telling all my tales of woe.

Yet in my dream I do not suffer,
Beseeching those on high
I heave a sigh
And in my sighing wake the dying,
Breathing in my breath of life.

And in my dream I have no heartache,
No passion to control.
I rest my soul
And in my resting wake the living
Praying loud my prayer of hope.

So in my dream I sense no sorrow,
No sadness to be seen.
I live to dream
And in my living wake the loving,
Dreaming of my dream of love.

1975

I HAD A DREAM

I had a vivid dream last night:
I went for a walk to take in the sights.
Streets and shops were mainly empty,
No crowds of people in a rush,
No one queuing for train or bus
But of things to do, there were plenty.

As there was no one else about
I went for a swim in the local river.
Once I was in I couldn't get out
So I went with the flow, all a-quiver.

Feeling all washed up, my spirits sank.
In time I was dumped on a muddy bank.
Not the best of places to be -
By now I was dying for a pee.
I hunkered down on bended knee
Then a dog strolled up and peed on me!

An owl flew past at a roundabout
And knocked me down with a feather.
When I stood up I rolled about
Like a ship in stormy weather.

At last I made it all the way home
And saw the folly of those who roam.
Around the silent streets at night,
I'd learnt enough to see the light.
It was a dreadful dream, I do confide,
Which seemed much worse when I revived.
I woke in my bed, feeling oh so guilty,
All dripping wet and really filthy.

25th February 2016

BEYOND OUR KEN (HAIKU)

Things exist which we
Don't hear, see, smell, taste or touch;
Our sixth sense says so.

8th December 2011

HANDS

Flesh
Bones
Blood
Nails
Digits
Pick up
Put down
Move around
Make a sound
Open wide
Try to hide
Throw aside
On a limb
Right and left
Inside out
Tell-tale lines
Reading palms
Join together
Making signs
Shaking
Hands.

1972

THE POTTER

The potter's wheel spins;
The potter, in control,
Moulds the clay
Gently with his hands
Giving form to shapes
Within his mind.

His mind, his hands, his wheel,
Work in unison,
In concentrated effort,
Developing skills to create
Precision and perfection
Out of nothing.

The potter is a useful being;
He helps us to see ourselves.
We too could imitate the potter
In motive, effort and deed;
Not making pots, but peace
And order out of chaos.

22nd January 1975

IN A SPIN

My shoes are on my feet
And my feet are on the ground.
The ground is on the Earth
And the Earth is spinning round.
Round and round the sun we go,
The sun in turn is turning.
Moving on and on we blow
Through boundless worlds of space.
The shoes upon my feet will rot.
What end the traveller waits?

6ᵗʰ June 1976

STARS

Stars are suns in the night.
Some are dead and some are bright.
They twinkle in the sky and give it light.
They offer hope of other forms of life.

The stars are company to our own,
In a universe which is our home,
Where one day man might freely roam.
Without them we'd be lonely and alone.

In billions of years our sun will die,
The human race will have to fly;
If all our hopes are to survive,
We need those suns to keep us starry-eyed.

13th December 1974

PERSPECTIVE

How far is a metre
To a snail?
How high is a hill
To an ant?
How great is a man
Compared to the Earth?
How small is our planet
Against the sun?
What size the sun
Compared to our galaxy,
Of which there are at least
A hundred thousand million others?
What size our galaxy
In the vast universe
Containing millions of other Milky Ways?
All parts must go
In proportion to the whole,
And we, a part,
Must find our own
Perspective.

1973

GLASS EYE

I stood by a pool, dazzling,
Like a window of glass
Reflecting the sun.
I looked in the mirror
Beyond the surface
At the cool depths below,
Where I saw darting fish
And plant-like forms
Swaying to and fro.
Each in its own way
Searching for food.
But for all I could see
The water was void.
A drop from that pool
Of clear water I took
And placed on a slide.
Then I had a close look
Through a more powerful
Mechanical glass eye.
And there, invisible before,
Were many strange creatures
Swimming about.
Without a doubt
There are more,
Micro- and macroscopic,
Which remain to be seen
Through the windows of life
By the 'blind' human eye.

1976

CARVE UP ON THE MOTORWAY

Steel sharp razor cars
Cut into the soft blotchy flesh of fog.

Ahead,
Pimples of red light
Stand out like familiar features of a face.

Taught hands tightly grip
The instruments of life and death,
Skilfully guiding them with surgeon-like precision,
Tracing the outline of the hard shoulder.

Laser beams of light converge,
Peeling the layers of skin
(Some thick, some thin)
Before incision.

Accidentally,
Knives meet sharply
Deep down inside the body.
Pools of blood slowly congeal in the still air.
For a time the flow stops
And the arterial road remains blocked
By the resulting embolism.

November 1975

IN LOVE WITH MY CAR

(With apologies to
Roger Taylor of Queen)

The machine is a dream
So clean,
With pistons pumping,
Hubcaps gleaming.
Holding the wheel
I steer with my hand
On the gear,
Throbbing with life
Racing along
In top.
Pulsating machine
Is well greased.
I've got a feel for my car
Like an obsession
And an addiction
Rolled into one.
It's a thrill
Driving my automobile.
Told my girl "goodbye"
For my four-wheeled friend
Never talks back
When I'm cruising in style,
Out to impress.

And later —
Cloth in hand,
I'm wiping it clean,
Gently polishing,
Caressing the sheen,
To mirror my face
In some masturbatory
Fantasy.
With my phallic symbol
I stand outside my door —
Steppenwolf would say
It was "For Ladies Only" —
Paying narcissistic homage.

1975

AT THE SILVER BLADES ICE RINK

Swirling figures in cold air
Sliding and gliding
Gracefully
Over the crispy surface
Of the hard ice.

Packs of people pick their way
Stumbling and tumbling
Seemingly
In a frenzied trance-like dance
Anti-clockwise.

Steel silver blades underfoot
Hissing and swishing
Constantly
Cutting round the glassy rink
Menacingly.

Occasional spills of blood
Slipping and tipping
Carelessly
With splinters of brittle bone
Cracked on impact.

July 1976

THE CLOT, ST. MARGARET'S HOSPITAL, EPPING

I remember the pain pulsating
With each sledgehammer blow
Against my chest -
And the panic
As I gulped for air
And coughed up lumps of blood
Instead.

It was night.
The ward was sleeping.
A single light
On the wall opposite
Cast shadows which were all a blur.
Out of time, floating,
Fragments of fact and fiction
Punctured projected images on my mind.
All I could hear
Was the soft hiss around my head
Of oxygen cylinders beside my bed.

At unknown intervals
I opened and closed my eyes.
Minutes? Hours? Days? Weeks? Months?
Maybe even years?
In and out of time
Dodging the random Reaper,
More by chance than design.

Conscious only of the mask about my face
And that slow continuous hiss
Of the pure life-saving gas
Travelling along some umbilical-like cord
From a placenta I could not turn my head to see.

My body racked, spread-eagled,
Feet slightly raised,
No pillow for my head,
Which spun confusingly
In a mist of uncertainty.

My lungs, blocked with clotted blood,
Heaved and strained, as in a tug-of-war,
To gain but whits of air.
Each gasp for breath
Choked in my throat
And gave a sense of drowning;
(where in the deep, the water fills you up
until you cannot take another drop,
but hit the bottom dead).
Sinking slowly into the dark
Unconscious depths of time and space
Once more
Wanting it to end.

Only to rise later,
Surfacing like some unsinkable cork.
Aware, a night nurse posted by my bed
Lightly held my hand.
The Sister rearranged the mask

Around my face
And wiped away my tears and sweat.
A smattering of conversations overheard:
"Pulse rate one-forty..."
"...his family been informed?"
"Yes Sister... shall I change the bottle over?"
"...in the right thigh I think..."
"Relations flying down... should be here soon."
"Maximum number of mills.... morphine..."
"...thank you nurse. The doctor's on his way."
"Pethidine..."

Fine flesh the needles stabbed like steel darts.
Punctured skin scabbed with blood...
The fight to save my life went on
With doctors reappearing.
Blood pressure count with pulse was checked
And record kept of breathing.
The pressure on my chest increased;
Crushed in a vice of granite rock
I could not move.
I waited for the final grip
To take its hold
And squeeze me,
Leave me,
Dead.

The night sped on.
I struggled in a stupor.
Whims and fancies filled my head
Of childhood days when all was red and rosy.

Alas my mind kept wandering.
Memories, as visions flashed by,
Brought back a sense of living.
Thoughts of home
And loved ones near and far
(I wished they could be nearer)
Became quite clear
And then would disappear.
I had a vision of my youth
As in some messy shorts and shirt
With muddy boots I scored a goal
And fell down in a puddle.

I slumped again into a state of bliss,
Oblivious to pain and suffering,
Knowing nothingness.
The night sped on
Its shadow hanging over me
As I hung on.
It dawned on me
If I should die —
Next second —
My loved ones would not know
And nor would I.
'Tis such a simple step
From one plane to the other.

And so it was I woke to find
The morning sun,
The crisis over
And the battle almost won

And all the fighters gone
Except for one;
Who lay as helpless as a new-born babe
Too weak to feed himself or raise his head,
With five more weeks to lie in bed
Before returning home.
The clot,
Anti-coagulated,
No more could stop
The rivers of life within.

1965

HOSPITAL FOOD AND
NEW BUILDING

Dear Chef of the Day
(Or Clerk of the Works)
We received with joy
Your little jest;
A brick for pud
Which was a treat
Though far too difficult to eat.
We were well on the mend
In peaceful Ward 5
Until we attacked
Your 'Concrete Surprise',
Then out came the teeth
Dented and broke
Trying to eat
Your Health Service joke.
Now we have lockjaw,
Gums that are sore,
Unable to speak,
We can't ask for more.
When rushed to the loo
From swallowing a morsel
We left our 'deposits',
The 'bricks' and the 'mortar'!
Is this how we play
Our part in the game,
By supplying the builders
Outside with the same?
Next time you cook

Can we please have a hammer
To break up the crust
In appropriate manner?
A fork and a spoon
Are really no use.
Better a drill,
Pneumatic of course!
Then all can appreciate
Your comical works,
As we lay in our beds
Enjoying 'the perks".

28th September 1985

A DIALOGUE WITH MATRON
(On the death of my father)

Who is that imposter in my father's bed?
He looks so ill. He seems half-dead.

It is your father and he is quite dead
He passed away just like I said.

O don't be daft. It's a waxwork dummy;
A sick joke I find not funny.

We thought it best to lay him out
In order to allay all doubt.

What happened to his bottom set of teeth?
His upper and lower lips don't meet.

We couldn't fix a smile upon his face
'Cause we found his dentures much too late.

But his mouth's half open like a fish
And he still feels warm and not quite stiff.

It can't be helped, we're short of staff.
To hunt for teeth? Don't make me laugh!

I know that Matron, but my father dear
Was much too nice to wear a sneer.

If that's the case, think not it's him
But an imposter of the man within.

I told you so. He is not dead.
That's only his shell upon the bed.

His mask of death looks so grotesque,
At least his soul is now at rest.

19th November 1997

FACE THE NATION

The face of England
Blotched and blighted,
Struck by the architects' plague.
That face which once was
So beautifully made
Is pock-marked by cities
And inflamed conurbations.
Villages and towns like festering sores
Expand with the economic need for more.
The stain of industry everywhere,
Spreading poisons, disease and grief,
Like eating away the leper's cheek;
Eyes smarting, nose running,
Ears aching, mouth gaping,
Skin cracking, oozing pus,
Smeared with the ointment 'pollution';
A product marketed by evolution
To hide the parasites feeding off the nation.

Oh, Merry England, weep no more!
Have a face-lift, find a cure.
Smile again with conservation
Or pay the price, decapitation.

1975

GRASS ROOTS

Friesians frozen on a landscape
Black and white on green.
Mamma mammals tapping pastures
Farming full of cream.
Devon milk and money flowing
Liquid paper round,
About the lush sleep of the suburbs
Floats a fluid sound.
Rattling rows of golden bottle tops
Wake dozing herds of flesh;
In glass houses pint-sized cows
Stand partly pasteurised fresh.

Inside a home at mother's breast
A baby seeks a nipple.
On heated stove the food of love
Simmers to a ripple:
Man cooing, cow mooing.
Outside, wet grass grows brittle.

This vision of a winter's morn
Fades with watching weathered eye.
While home-delivered milk is mourned
Mounds of concrete and brick sprout high.
Panoramas blotched by angled roofs
Blot verdant fields blood red.
New livestock in designer boots, not hoofs,
Trample underfoot with careless tread
Young shoots of grass once free to spread
Which now lie dead beneath grey stone beds;
Ground on which fresh human herds will soon be bred.

1972

CHARD SUNSET

Glorious glow of the descending sun
With golden puffs floating across
The darkening sky.
Smoke from a garden bonfire hangs
Suspended in a leaning spiral
Tapering to a tip.
Silver bird with vapour trail
Silently sweeps across the copper hue,
Painting an ormolu streak,
Which runs unblended on the horizon.

High above the town
Trees stand to attention, like sentries,
Silhouetted against the sunset,
Guarding the ridge to Snowdon Hill.

To the east, the heavens already sparkle;
Blue-black velvet spangled with stars,
Dressed for night, by a wave
From Tinkerbell's magic wand.
Beneath, in cathedral silence,
Lies the town in a crystal bowl;
A study of still life,
Lit by the embers of a dying fire.

1975

BONFIRE NIGHT

Guy Fawkes, maverick of British law,
Burning on the seat of justice,
Surrounded by salamanders
Spitting their lizard-tongue forks of fire;
The fall-guy falls as usual, cremated.
Spirits dance in the pyramid of flames;
Blue, orange, yellow flickers,
Throwing sparks into the sky.
Crackles mingle with the laughter
Of the people standing by.
Children waving sparklers,
Faces shining with delight.
Fireworks banging, popping, fizzing,
Rockets zooming through the night.
Catherine-wheels whizzing round,
Shooting stars falling to the ground.
Silver fountains cascading lights;
Roman candles, red, green and white.
Treacle toffee, parkin, jacket-potatoes,
Consumed like the guy
By the traditional bonfire.

5th November 1975

NUCLEAR POWER

A speck slits the blue
Silk of sky swiftly falling
Like a dart to earth.

People cowering
Watch with fearful eyes praying
For a miracle.

The missile hangs in
The air above the quiet
Cathedral suspense.

A dot hits the ground
Frozen in a streak like an
Exclamation mark.

Full-stop silence as
Petrified parents think last
Thoughts before the flash.

Brilliant white hot
Light too bright to face hides the
Growing mushroom cloud.

The blast-rush of wind
Scorches eyes out of sockets
With its kiss of death.

Somewhere a puppet
Psychopathic push-button
President half-smiles.

1974

THE VALLEY OF THE LIVING DEAD

As I walk through the valley of the living dead,
I see the blind who cannot see the light.
I watch the deaf who cannot hear the word.
I meet the dumb who cannot talk.
Having eyes to see and ears to hear and tongues to speak
They have not learned to use their senses,
So they dwell in the valley of the living dead.
Pathetic cases of their own creation
Gathering round their shallow souls
Material possessions to fill their lives.
All hopes are based on false elation
Manufactured to create sensation,
Only to find they are bent and broken
As they walk through the valley of the living dead.
The poet who has lost his rhyme,
The minstrel who has lost his song,
The preacher who has lost his faith,
All hope that someone else will lend a hand
When finding signs they do not understand.
The scientist who lacks imagination,
The proud who strive to keep their reputation,
All are walking through the valley of the living dead.
They know not why they live.
They work to buy their happiness,
All slaves to ownership.
They flaunt their artificial beauty
Which by money they possess,
Hoping all who view their gains will feel deprived

And like them, will want for more.
Yet all the time they are slowly dying
As they walk through the valley of the living dead.
People come and people go while time ticks on.
Some have a daughter, some a son.
From all the truths of life they run.
Ignorance multiplies their guilt;
Their minds they cannot mend,
Their love they cannot share,
Their hearts are empty, bare.
Colourless characters, eyes completely blank,
With naked personalities stand
Lined up in order hand in hand
Along the valley of the living dead.

Cut short my visit to this place
Where millions gather to perform
Their roles in life unto its end.
They live, yet all the time pretend
To be what they are not.
This confused and ugly lot
Are driving me insane.
Spare me the pain
Of watching them rot
In the valley of the living dead.
Dear God, on whom I call,
I do not know you much at all.
I thought I did, but then the darkness came
And clouded up my cluttered brain.
Why did you lead me to this place?

Was it to understand your grace?
Release me now and let me live.
The light is bright and crystal clear.
The mist inside my head is lifting.
My eyes are moist with joy,
My freedom now I will enjoy
And new-found knowledge I'll employ
In helping those who do not use their senses
To appreciate the wonder of the world
Outside the valley of the living dead.

1968

HAPPINESS

Happiness is like an elusive shadow,
Needing contrast, dark and light,
To give it form
And people to make it viable.

Happiness can be bought.
Like an unwilling slave,
It will work for a while
Then disappear with
Diminishing appreciation;
Desire having secured the escape
By loosening the chains of bondage.

Happiness can be taught
By punishment and reward
In the school of ambition.
Motivated by discontent
It becomes an ideal;
An aim to be realised
Through suffering and deprivation.

Happiness can be sought,
But to seek we first
Must discover the clue
To its ultimate source.
The more we look
The less we'll be satisfied.
For we cannot find it - it finds us.

Happiness can be caught.
It is infectious and spreads
With our caring and sharing.
We cannot contain it,
We cannot retain it.
We receive more if we pass it on,
For happiness is essentially free.

1976

ON BEING HUMAN

Oh Great Designer in the sky
May I ask the question Why?
When you devised the means
By which we propagate our genes,
Were you not entirely sober?
Or suffering a hangover?
It's a comical process which starts
I must confess, in physical farce.
Alas it ends in pointless pain.
Birth is messy, uncomfortable, a strain;
Agony for Mum and harrowing for Dad.
Potentially dangerous. You must be mad!
Was there really no other way
To secure our human progeny?

Unstable and many would say unsafe,
Our home is a planet with tectonic plates;

Volcanic eruptions, earthquakes and floods
(All provided by the One who loves?)
Shifting like sand deciding our fates.
Is this what's best for the human race?
When God made the Earth, He said it was good,
Yet most would rebuild it, if only they could.
We seek out cures for our social ills
And push the limits of medical skills.
For everything there is a time and place;
Maybe like nomads we are meant to roam
And secure ourselves a safer home
Somewhere out there in boundless space.

19th August 2013

THE LOST TRIBES

We know the whereabouts of Benjamin and Judah
But where are the missing ten lost tribes?
And what of the promises made by God to Israel,
Are they null and void? Did they not survive?

Did the tribes migrate across the whole of Europe
Then settle in these far off western isles?
Did their descendants take the Word of God to others
Spreading faith and hope to enlighten lives?

Did the Anglo-Saxon Celtic-speaking nations
Fit the role of a chosen people?
And when called upon to suffer sacrifice and loss,
Did they boast about it from church steeples?

Was Joseph of Arimathea the first to plant the seed
In this outpost of the Roman Empire,
By bringing Jesus at the age of twelve to live here,
As holy writ and legend so conspire?

Is God working out his purpose each successive year?
As a nation, do we have a choice?
If so, our history and our future path are clear -
As spoken by the prophets with one voice.

20th March 2016

KING ARTHUR

King Arthur was of lowly birth
He was by Merlin made,
Tintagel Castle was his home
And fighting was his trade.
He fought the Saxons and the Scots,
He sought the Holy Grail.
He held his court at Camelot
With knights so bold and brave.

King Arthur was a Cornishman
And noble were his aims.
He ruled with Guinevere his queen
And for her beauty paid.
He fought the Irish and the Danes,
He sought the Holy Grail,
Merlin made him a magic sword,
Excalibur by name.

King Arthur beat his enemies
And never made them slaves.
He taught them justice with his sword
And freedom freely gave.
He fought the Romans and the French,
He sought the Holy Grail.
His knights were faithful, but alas
Was by his wife betrayed.

King Arthur went away to fight
And left his queen to reign.
His nephew Mordred came one night
And with the queen did lay.
As soon as Arthur and his knights
Were told the sorry tale
They journeyed home to save the throne
And Mordred he was slain.

King Arthur took a mortal wound,
His body racked with pain.
They carried him to Avalon,
His life they tried to save.
His queen sought refuge as a nun,
He sought the Holy Grail.
The Cup of Christ he came to sup
Then rested in his grave.

1971

THE ONE AND ONLY

On my journey home
I passed by way of Laugharne
And there
Along the Cliff Road
I came upon a boathouse
Where for fifteen years
Until his death in '53
Lived the "one and only"
Welsh bard.
Alas
I could not enter
The garden nor the house
For the cost
Was more than I could raise.
I consoled myself
By taking in the panoramic views
Across the estuary of the Taf
As he had done
A thousand times before.
I wandered back
Along the lane
And found the simple wooden shed -
His sanctuary -
Where he had written
Millions of words
With poor reward
Which still survive
Though he is dead.

Further on along the lane
A man
Well on in years
Was seated on a wall
Resting from his brushing up
And hedgerow cutting.
As l passed by
He smiled
And greeted me
A cheery "Good day".
I stopped in my tracks.
He touched his cloth cap.
I replied in kind
And asked if he knew
The way to the grave
Where the great man lay.
"Aye" said the old man,
"I knew him well, poor boy.
Such a nice boy he was too.
Used to walk down this lane here.
Saw him almost every day.
Moody he was too.
Sometimes he'd be full of the joys of spring
And stop and pass the time of day.
Talk for hours he would.
Other times
He'd pass by
And ne'er speak a word.

Shy, see.
Sensitive too.
Pity he had to die
To be famous.
When he was alive
Never had two pennies to rub together
He didn't.
No...
All that business
About him being an alcoholic -
Absolute rubbish, see.
Never had enough money for drink
All a myth.

Oh aye
'Twas the drink that killed him though.
Drank a bottle and a half of whiskey
So they say.
Would have killed the strongest man.
Only thirty-six he was too.
Nobody ever heard of him
When he was alive.
Then they started coming
In the summer
After he'd gone.
Pilgrims.
Now they come
Summer and winter
From all over the world.
Had a girl of sixteen here the other day.

Come over from Canada
She did.
Said she hitch-hiked all the way.
No wonder there's so many murders about.
Ask for it
Some of 'em do."

He leaned on his walking stick
Bent like his legs
Riddled with arthritis.
His big brown eyes
Moistened a little
As they stared at me
In vacant expression.
"Aye" he muttered
As if to himself.
"Pity he had to die like that
To get famous.
Buried in the churchyard he is
Out on the St. Clears road.
If you go that way
On your right
You'll see St. Martin's church.
There's a car park there.
You'll find some steps going up.
Go up the steps
And 'cross the bridge.
There, on the other side
In the centre of the field
Is a simple wooden cross.

Painted white, it is.
Surrounded by great marble
tombstones
In memory of others.
It's the only wooden cross there.
Too poor for a proper headstone, see.
That's where you'll find
The one and only."
I thanked the old man
And he shook me by the hand.
"Aye" he sighed
As I went on my way.

9th August 1975

MYSELF

I'm inclined to be good and inclined to be bad.
I'm usually happy but sometimes I'm sad.
I try to do good but so often I fail.
I'm undoubtedly witty, but my wit can grow stale.

Some call me a fool, others say that I'm wise.
I'm probably both but they don't realise
The fact that we're all a little of each.
Perfection is something quite out of our reach.

They say I'm eccentric, it's true, I can tell.
One moment in heaven, the next I'm in hell.
I tend to be cautious and common with sense.
I'm very understanding, but sometimes I'm dense.

Occasionally, I'm stupid and very unwise.
I'm usually honest but I sometimes tell lies.
I'm very observant and seldom forget
The moments of pleasure with people I've met.

I'm extremely obliging, respectful and kind.
I never shoot dogs or people who are blind.
I'm very considerate as you can well see.
Although I forget things, I've a good memory.

Independent, yet faithful, and loyal till the end,
I'm a perfect companion to stranger or friend.
Yet proud and conceited, I'm humble and low,
Sarcastic and lazy, untidy and slow.

I'm a likeable person as everyone knows;
Me, most of all, as each moment it grows -
My liking myself that little bit more -
Good on the surface but bad to the core.

1960

A SIMPLE MAN

I am a simple man at heart
Who enjoys the occasional fart;
For farts are fun and simply made,
Pure air their pungent smells pervade.
Some are silent, others loud,
Some disperse a gathered crowd.
Unique in pitch as well as pong
I like them more than any song.
When in the bath we liberate
And bubbles blown reverberate.
When bursting forth in packed-out room
They break the boredom or the gloom,
Causing folk to glance and titter,
Keen to see who has the jitters.
Light a match and you will find
A blue flash leads to burnt behind.
Guilty party flushed with shame
Departs head down to fart again.
To those uncultured in the arts,
The most expressive is to fart.
To a simple man it's all too plain,
No two farts are e'er the same.

6th August 1996

COMING TO TERMS

My parents confessed I was an accident
Conceived amid bombs at the height of war.
They already had three. Didn't want any more.

They said they would have preferred a girl.
They liked the names Rosalind and Rose,
To suit a wished-for scholar or lover of prose.

In fact my talents lay in the field of sport.
No family members ever came to watch me play;
"A grammar education going to waste" they'd say.

When I 'got religion' I applied to be ordained.
I quite fancied being a padre or a preacher.
The Church denied me, so I ended up a teacher.

My wife would wish me to be a practical man;
A maker and mender, helper and cleaner,
Not someone who spends his day a dreamer.

I have two lovely irreplaceable daughters
But always yearned for a companionable son.
I was told that three is unlucky for some.

Let nothing mean too much when testing Fate.
It's said that those who want will never get;
Like when we pray for sun it turns out wet.
Desire and denial, with familiar ring,
Resonate throughout our capricious lives.
Not a thing about which to rejoice or sing,
More a warning bell of what the future brings.

4ᵗʰ October 2013

WATCHING THE
SUN SET

The Sun
       is setting
The Sky
       is darkening
The Air
       is chilling
The Mist
       is rising
The Birds
       are silent
The Trees
       are still
The Lovers
       are sleeping
The Day
       is over
And I am
       one step nearer
My Journey's
       End.

1977

LIFE'S JOURNEY

I remember I crawled with limited sight.
When I was a babe I was vaguely aware
There was much more to see from high in the air.
When I was lifted I glimpsed for a time
Horizons far distant, great heights to be mine.

At length I stood up and finally walked.
I saw the world from a much higher plane
With risks and gambles you find in a game.
There were trees, high hills, steep cliffs, above all –
Social ladders to climb from which I could fall.

I longed for the day when I could proceed
To ascend the mountains, their beauty to view.
The world diminished the larger I grew,
So I set my sights on goals I could reach
And believed I had the world at my feet.

As an adult I ran with abandoned haste.
Intent on my goals, I missed much on the way
Yet some things I saw which remain to this day.
The journey, so easy as it first appeared,
Proved longer and harder than ever I'd feared.

Meandering on, my progress was checked:
Obstructions, delays, disasters and loss;
Deep gorges, steep slopes, swift rivers to cross.
Companions I joined gave help and good cheer,
My hardships, though shared, grew harder each year.

A kind word, a smile, a wave on the way;
At last a breather gave chance to look back
To see my children retracing my tracks.
What once was so near now seemed afar off;
One rests more often approaching the top.

My legs wore weary towards journey's end.
The panorama clearer, nearer the peak;
New challenges proved more difficult to meet.
I saw the mistakes which I made in my past -
I wasn't the first and I'll not be the last.

The sun which sets in the warm western sky
Will rise in the east at the breaking of dawn.
With night drawing on I must wait till the morn,
Then the summit I'll reach and take in the view.
On the other side await pastures new.

1978

LAST ORDERS

Grieve not for me when I am gone
But fill your heart and mind with song.
Mope not nor hang your head for long
But gird your loins and journey on.

Our bodies were not made to last.
I'm stuck with mine until it's ash!
For me the future is now past.
What of my soul? I dare not ask.

Remember me, a part of you;
Hand in hand we stretched and grew,
Bonded by values shared by few,
Weaned on love in a family pew.

Be thankful for each gifted year.
Rejoice and hold each moment dear.
Treat death itself as nought to fear
And wipe away all mournful tears.

We march through history marking time
And one by one drop out of line.
Your turn will come just as has mine
So celebrate your life in kind,
Enjoy my wake, fine food and wine.

26th July 2005

ACKNOWLEDGEMENTS

I wish to say a big THANK YOU to all those people who, both recently and over the years, have selected these poems as their favourites. In alphabetical order but with equal appreciation: Ken Bamford, Suzanne Bamford, Jenny Bevan, Jean Breeze, Lindsay Burnett, Thelma Clarke, Josie Cook, Samantha Cook, Dr A.J. Dalzell-Ward, John Denness, Derek English, Josie Gatley, Kate Geraghty, Nancy Harling, Carole Hill, John Hind, Teresa Howlett, Libby Holder, Phil Holder, Tricia Jardine, Daniel Lissett, Ian MacLean, Patricia Martin, Patrick Martin, Lucy Mills, Sophie Mills, Trudy Nazer, Robin Schaefli, George Smith, Janet Stewart, Nancy Stokes, Robert Wain, Bill Watson, Joan Watson, Joan Wedgwood, and last but not least Virtual Admin UK, for typing so diligently the original manuscript. My sincerest apologies to anyone I may have omitted unwittingly.

M.J.C.

APPENDIX

Books in which the above poems were first published

STEPPING STONES

Education
Friends
Love
Perspective
Questions About Life
School
School Cat
The Four Seasons
The Knock Upon Your Door
The Potter
The Valley Of The Living Dead
Time
When You Are Gone
Where Were You?

REFLECTING IN THE SUN

Alone, Reflecting In The Sun
At Lyme Regis
Bonfire Night
Carve Up On The Motorway
Face The Nation
Happiness
Little Children
Take The Sun

COLLECTED POEMS 1959–2014

REVIEWS AND COMMENTS

About *Stepping Stones*: "The reader is in for a pleasant surprise, for the poems are not only for those who are very deep in literature but also for the layman. I find in him a subtlety that is hard to come across within the scope of modern poets. Moreover, the poet has not tried to stereotype himself into a certain mould. Rather, he has tried to keep all avenues open and let his imagination run wild with deep thought and analysis. The depth in these poems shows that they are the brainchild of an artist." – Jagdish Bhatt, Current Events, *India's National Journal on World Affairs* (Vol XXII No. 10 November 1976).

"Here within its covers are the winged thoughts of one who has felt the compulsion and exercised the necessary discipline to write poems; and also known the delight and the despair of the creation. He is young in spirit as all poets are and has the flame of the denunciatory fire of youth. I enjoyed these poems and deeply appreciated the compelling drive behind them. Michael Cook feels strongly about certain problems in modern life, questioning in a simple direct way those aspects which are the concern of us all." – Muriel Hilton, *The Inquirer* (31st January 1976).

"I'm very attracted by the clarity and precision you go for, as well as a very proper density of thought behind the writing. I'd like to put on a reading of 'Questions' at one of our school assemblies – splendid dialogue, very skilfully and sensitively done." – Charles Causley, the Cornish poet and teacher (in a letter to the author dated 12th January 1976).

"I like the poems immensely and have read through the

book many times with increasing pleasure and enjoyment."
– G.N.G. Smith, Vice Principal, Bede College, University of
Durham (in a letter to the author dated 9th December 1975).

"A fine, thought-provoking achievement." – Paul King,
Devon C.C. Adviser for Religious Education.

About *Reflecting In The Sun*: "I greatly enjoyed reading it
for its qualities of clarity and directness. Once again, the
poems really communicate. I think the new book a real
advance on the earlier one – much as I liked it." Charles
Causley, the Cornish poet and teacher (in a letter to the
author dated 7th November 1976).

"The depth of these poems shows that they are the
brainchild of an artist." – Jagdish Bhatt, Dehra Dun, India.

"Powerful and consistent... some effective, if chilling
poems." – *The Countryman*.

"His enthusiasms, despairs, his voice of denunciation were
heard in many of his poems and in the keenly critical eye
with which he observes so much that despoils modern life" -
Muriel Hilton, *The Inquirer* (23rd October 1976).

About *Of Faith And Fortune*: "He has begun to emerge as
a poet of some stature." -*Pulman's Weekly News*, Devon and
Dorset editions, 19th July 1977.

"That he is talented is undeniable and he is recognised as
one of the best of the new generation of poets." - *The Western
Gazette*, 22nd July 1977.

"All the poems are of the same high calibre." – *Stockport
Express and Advertiser*.

"His inquiring mind travels over a variety of interests and
in his direct, simple manner he communicates his
experiences, ideas and the values which dominate his life. He
has a keen observant eye and sees life with a certain humour,

though he is deeply conscious of its pathos and tragedy. His poems have the great advantage of being easily understood" – Muriel Hilton, *The Inquirer* (14th January 1978).

"I've enjoyed it very much... the energy and vitality at the imaginative source of such work will not allow you to leave things there. I like too the very evident way in which the poems spring from the experiences of everyday living. The Laugharne poem, *In A Spin, Drink To Me Only*, The Clot poem and particularly *Tree Speech* are just some of the pieces I found very moving and memorable... *A Lesson* – marvellously observed and caught." – Charles Causley, the Cornish poet and teacher (in a letter to the author dated 24th July 1977).

About *O Didaskalos*: "Apparently the title means Teacher in the New Testament Greek, which seems appropriate to this collection of modern poetry and its diversity of themes, forms and styles of rhyming/non-rhyming verse, thus making it suitable for use as a teaching guide for students of the art. The subject range is vast. Relayed in enthusiastic, comic or melancholic mode, with many having been published previously in mags and anthologies, help to make this most readable." – Ken M. Ellison in *New Hope International Review* (Vol 20, 1998).

"This volume of verse, though daunting to some with its title, provides an accessible, varied fare of themes and moods and gives a fascinating eye-opener into the breadth and depth of the author's world. Observations, social comment, abound; also many unanswered questions. Like any good teacher, he challenges the reader/pupil to think for him/herself. The main purpose of presenting hefty themes in digestibly compact rhythmic forms is admirably carried out. An arid humour pervades much of the writing. Because of the alphabetical arrangement, love poems appear, surprisingly and delightfully like scatter-cushions; but never exclusive to the context of the outer world (or indeed the universe). Some poems are deeply personal yet leave room for a wider philosophy." – Felicia Houssein, *Christian Poetry Review* (Number 7, July 1997).

"The varied subject matter of this enjoyable collection makes it a useful book for teachers looking for a teaching guide. Among poems about cricket, pussycats, nuclear power, typing, dropouts, the NHS, seal culls, senses, school, children to name but a few, there is the very human *Myself*... Scattered among these are Michael Cook's best – his poems of love and lost love." – Frank Clarke, *The Teacher* (November 1997).

"l am inspired by all your fantastic poems" – Paige Burgess.

"I did enjoy your book, I think your book is really good" – Max Higgins.

"I really enjoyed your book" – Louis Wright.

"I think your poems are great" – Charlotte Cook.

(Comments of pupils at Stockport School (in a letter to the author dated December 2014).

"The poems I felt worked best were usually amongst the shorter items. Poems such as *At The Silver Blades Ice Rink*, a purely descriptive piece but one where the words flow as easily as the skaters... poems like *Getting Nowhere* and *lnertia*: short, succinct, to the point. You get a lot for your money." – George Ruggles, *Target Five Part Two* (January 1998).

"For the lovers of verse this book is a must, but even if you think you don't understand poetry there is bound to be something here which makes you laugh, cry or just wonder... it's well worth the money." Sheila Hewitt, *Kirkby Mallory News No 8* (Easter 1997).

"O Didaskalos contains a fascinating collection of poems... there is something for everyone to take away from these poems. There is something to be gained in reading them not all at once but a few at a time. The writer obviously has an appreciation of language and the rhythms of language. There is so much meaning bursting out of each stanza." – Jane Evans, Minerva Press (25th March 1996).

"An aptly titled collection of thought-provoking verse from a skilful writer." – Alpine Press.

"The author of this disciplined collection has a refreshing approach to writing which turns the accepted concept of the precocious poet on its head... a variety of styles have been successfully approached to highlight complex constructions, difficult metres, a particular number of syllables per line and intricate rhyme schemes which makes the anthology a useful teaching manual." Lea Evans, *The Hinckley Times* (13th February 1997).

About *Collected Poems 1959-2014*: "The intention of this collection is to provide something for everyone. I think it does. This is what amounts to be Mr. Cook's life's work, half a century of writing poetry, man and boy. It's fair to say that the author is someone unafraid to try practically anything poetic. There are 207 poems in this collection. I'm not going to guess how many different forms were included. There are 14 different types listed on the back cover alone... there are poems in a very traditional style here, poems that (gasp!) rhyme, there may even be some traditional values. There is a lot of ambition here. Does it pay off? Yes it does. Reading this book feels like walking through a festival field and getting snatches of lots of different things, without any of them dominating, apart from the voice of the organiser." – Andrew Barber, *Pulsar Poetry Webzine #24* (September 2015).

"The poet has combined a series of styles and topics throughout his life, thoughts and experiences. After a serious knee injury that was to stop him from playing football for the rest of his life, a new poet was born and published in anthologies, magazines and newspapers. A very well-published volume." – *Dandelion Arts Magazine*, London (March 2016).

"Highly enjoyable to anyone who is a devotee of poetry but also beneficial to those who are not much acquainted with this limb of the arts. The vast majority of poems have nothing to do with sport... but where there are some they are like most of the work, by turns amusing or serious. In terms of football there is *Soccer Girl*, the story of a true fanatic, whilst *Georgie* is about George Best. Then *United* takes in change of events and *Offside* is a sad tale. Add a couple of cricket poems and a modicum of other pastimes, the rest is as diverse as can be imagined. However, the final poem is an emotional one concerning how to face death, entitled *Last Orders*, which would serve as a memorial for almost anyone." – *Coaching News*, London Football Coaches Association (29th July 2015).